Wales

Wales

BY LIZ SONNEBORN

Enchantment of the World™
Second Series

Frontispiece: **Houses in Tenby, Pembrokeshire**

Consultant: Robert Austin, PhD, Associate Professor, Centre for European, Russian and Eurasian Studies, University of Toronto, Toronto, Ontario

Please note: All statistics are as up-to-date as possible at the time of publication.

Book production by The Design Lab

Library of Congress Cataloging-in-Publication Data
Names: Sonneborn, Liz, author.
Title: Wales / by Liz Sonneborn.
Description: New York, NY : Children's Press, an Imprint of Scholastic, 2018.
  | Series: Enchantment of the world | Includes bibliographical references
  and index.
Identifiers: LCCN 2017028548 | ISBN 9780531235928 (library binding)
Subjects: LCSH: Wales—Juvenile literature.
Classification: LCC DA708 .S66 2018 | DDC 942.9—dc23
LC record available at https://lccn.loc.gov/2017028548

Scholastic Inc., 557 Broadway, New York, NY 10012

1 2 3 4 5 6 7 8 9 10 R 27 26 25 24 23 22 21 20 19 18

Welsh pony

Contents

Left to right: **Gower Peninsula, Brecon Beacons National Park, puffins, Tintern Abbey, sheep**

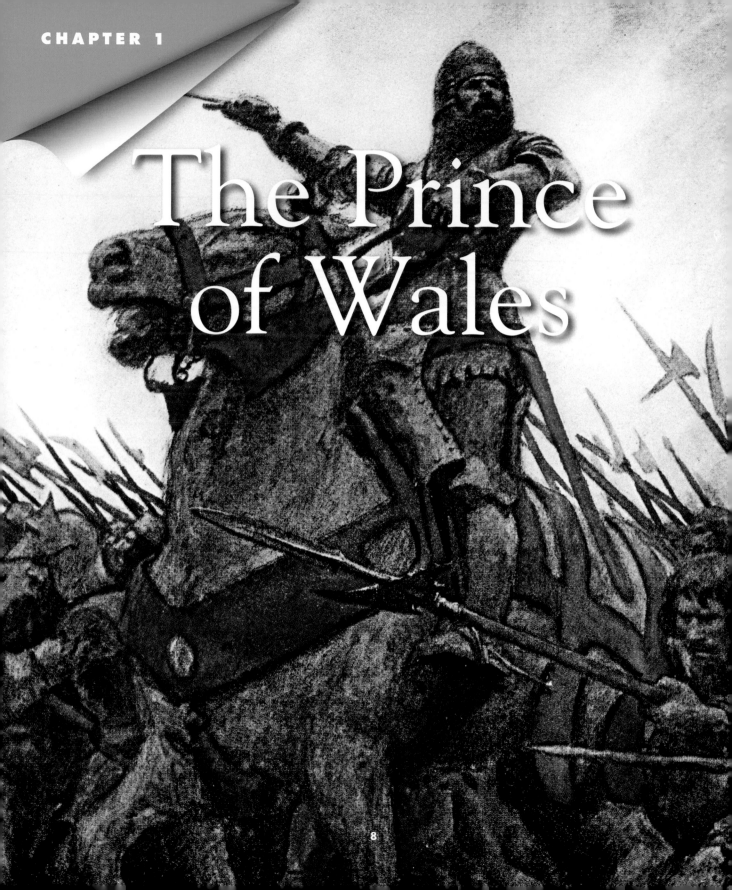

CHAPTER 1

The Prince of Wales

ON SEPTEMBER 16, 1400, OWAIN GLYNDWR gathered friends and family at his estate. Before the crowd, he made an outrageous, even dangerous declaration. Glyndwr named himself the true Prince of Wales.

The country of Wales is located on the western side of the island of Great Britain in Europe. Directly to the east of Wales lies England. When Glyndwr made his declaration, Wales had been controlled by England for more than a hundred years. After the English took control, the title of Prince of Wales no longer belonged to the Welsh, the people of Wales. It was now bestowed on the eldest son of the king of England.

By announcing that he was the Prince of Wales, Glyndwr was openly defying the English king. He was also lighting the spark that would inflame a rebellion.

Opposite: **Owain Glyndwr led thousands of men in his revolt against the English.**

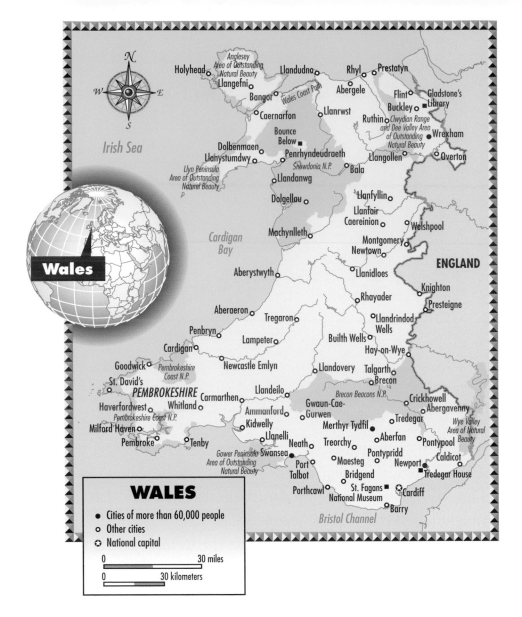

Defying the King

Born in about 1350, Glyndwr came from a distinguished Welsh family that lived near the English border. He was comfortable in English society. Glyndwr had spent time in the English capital of London. He had also served in the king's army.

So why did Glyndwr suddenly decide to challenge the

The land in Wales is a mix of rocky mountains and rolling hills.

king? He may have been angry because the king had not made him a knight and given him the privileges that came with that honor. Glyndwr may have been upset that the king did not come to his aid in a dispute with an English landowner. Or he may have just seen that the time was right to seize power.

Dreams of a Free Wales

Glyndwr knew that the Welsh people were unhappy being under England's thumb. The Welsh were desperately poor and felt exploited by the English. The English looked down on them and restricted their rights. The Welsh felt like second-class citizens in their own country.

Many old Welsh stories told of princes who had ruled Wales long ago. Glyndwr imagined himself as a leader in their mold. As Prince of Wales, he believed he could rally his beleaguered people and restore his nation to its former glory.

Conwy Castle was built between 1283 and 1289. It is considered one of the finest fortresses in Europe.

Clever and charismatic, Glyndwr amassed a small army. His men began attacking English towns in northeast Wales. But the rebellion's greatest early success came on April 1, 1401. Two cousins of Glyndwr's led a force of forty men in taking over Conwy Castle.

The attack had great symbolic meaning to the Welsh. The English had built castles all over Wales. The soldiers stationed there were charged with keeping the Welsh in line. Taking over one of the grandest castles with so few men impressed the Welsh. They began to think that perhaps somehow Glyndwr's rebellion might actually succeed.

Glyndwr's men mostly staged quick raids and surprise attacks. But on June 22, 1402, they met the English army in a full-fledged battle. To the shock of everyone, Glyndwr's ragged troops managed to defeat the professional English force.

Word of the great victory spread. More and more Welshmen joined the fight. By the summer of 1403, Glyndwr's forces had gained a hold over nearly every region in Wales.

A Welsh Hero

Glyndwr's army had some amazing victories, but it was no match for the English forces in the long run. Low on supplies and weapons, the tide started turning against Glyndwr and the Welsh army. The English took back Wales, bit by bit. By 1408, the Welsh had lost control of every part of the country.

In 1404, Owain Glyndwr formed a parliament, a law-making body. Creating a Welsh parliament was an important step toward creating an independent Wales.

Many of Glyndwr's supporters were killed, but he managed to escape.

Pockets of resistance continued to fight the English, but the rebellion slowly petered out. The Welsh resigned themselves once again to English rule, yet they remained true to Glyndwr.

Glyndwr lived out his life as a fugitive, hiding in caves and forests. No Welsh person, however, gave him up to the authorities. In 1415, one chronicler wrote, "Many say that he died, but the prophets say that he did not die."

Welsh people relax at a café in Cardiff. Many people in Wales identify themselves as Welsh rather than as both Welsh and British.

And these prophets were in a sense correct. Glyndwr the man might have died, but his legend lives on. In fact, the people of Wales now celebrate him as a national hero.

Revering Glyndwr

In the six hundred years since Glyndwr's rebellion, Wales has not won the independence it dreamed of. It is part of the United Kingdom, a country made up of Wales, England, Scotland, and Northern Ireland. In some ways, Wales is also still under England's shadow. Throughout their history, the Welsh have often felt resentment toward the English. Even though they share a country, the Welsh sometimes complain that the English do not respect them or take their concerns seriously.

United Kingdom

Glyndwr may have failed in his mission to create a free Wales, but the Welsh still hold him in high regard because he embodied so many of the qualities they revere. He was a bold and fearless leader, unwilling to back down no matter what. He was an underdog who, with grit and determination, dared to defy wealthy and powerful enemies. And most of all, he was a proud Welshman who was willing to fight and die for his land and his people.

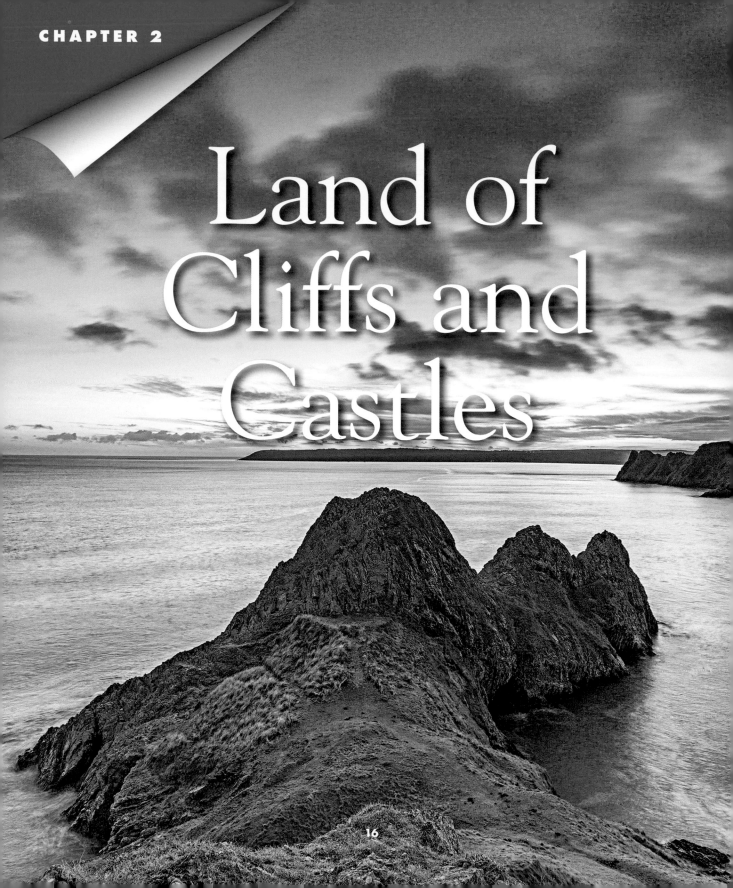

CHAPTER 2

Land of Cliffs and Castles

LOOK AROUND IN WALES AND YOU WILL SEE beautiful landscapes. The nation has high mountains, lush woods, spectacular waterfalls, and golden beaches. Perhaps Wales is best known for its rough and rugged coastline, where crystal blue waves dash into the sides of rocky cliffs.

Opposite: **A narrow strip of land juts into the sea near Swansea, in southern Wales.**

Geographic Features of Wales

Area: 8,015 square miles (20,759 sq km)

Highest Elevation: Mount Snowdon, 3,556 feet (1,084 m)

Length of Border with England: 160 miles (257 km)

Largest Island: Anglesey, 261 square miles (676 sq km)

Longest River: Severn, 220 miles (354 km)

Largest Lake: Bala Lake, 1.9 square miles (4.9 sq km)

Largest Reservoir: Lake Vyrnwy, 1.7 square miles (4.4 sq km)

Largest National Park: Snowdonia National Park, 838 square miles (2,170 sq km)

Average Daily High Temperature: In Cardiff, 47°F (8°C) in January, 71°F (22°C) in July

Average Daily Low Temperature: In Cardiff, 36°F (2°C) in January, 56°F (13°C) in July

Average Annual Precipitation: 50 inches (127 cm)

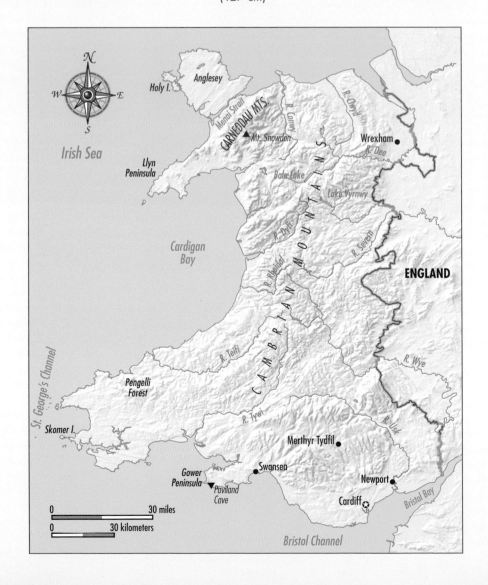

Where in the World Is Wales?

Wales is a small country located in western Europe, on the western edge of the island of Great Britain. Great Britain also includes Scotland and England. Wales's only land border is with England, which is situated directly to the east.

The rest of Wales is bound by water. To the north is the Irish Sea, which lies between Wales and the island of Ireland. To the west is Cardigan Bay and St. George's Channel. And to the south is the Bristol Channel.

Several islands are considered part of Wales. Anglesey is the largest. Located just off the northwest coast, it is separated from the mainland by the Menai Strait. Today, Anglesey and the mainland are linked by two bridges.

Many lighthouses were built along the Welsh coast to warn ships of the rocky land.

Offa's Dyke

In the late eighth century, Offa was the Saxon king of Mercia, located in what is now western England. He was wary of the rowdy rival rulers to the west in present-day Wales. To protect his land, he ordered an ambitious building project. He had his subjects build a wall of earth that marked the boundary between his realm and neighboring Welsh kingdoms. The long border wall became known as Offa's Dyke.

In many places, Offa's Dyke runs along the present-day border of Wales and England. The Welsh still sometimes refer to England using the phrase "beyond Offa's Dyke." The ancient earthwork is preserved today as the Offa's Dyke Path. On this national trail, hikers can take in some of the most beautiful scenery of both countries.

Spreading over 8,015 square miles (20,759 square kilometers), Wales is a little smaller than the state of New Jersey. Wales is the second-smallest nation in the United Kingdom, after Northern Ireland. Scotland is more than three times larger than Wales; England, more than five times larger. Wales includes just over 9 percent the United Kingdom's total land base.

Mountains, Rivers, and Lakes

Much of Wales is covered by hills and mountains. The Cambrian Mountains run like a backbone down the nation's center. The highest peaks of the Cambrian range are found in the Snowdonia area to the northwest. The tallest mountain in Wales is the rugged and rocky Mount Snowdon, which rises to the height of 3,556 feet (1,084 meters). It is the third-highest mountain in the United Kingdom.

Lowlands are mostly found on the island of Anglesey and in the region near the English border. There are also sandy beaches in the north and west of Wales. Resorts there attract tourists from England and the rest of Europe who come to enjoy the sand and scenery. Much of the coastline is also marked by soaring cliffs.

Low-lying areas also include the bottom of deep river valleys. The rivers of Wales include the Dee in the north, the Clwyd in the northeast, and Rheidol in the west. The nation's two longest rivers are found in the southeast. The Severn

Towering cliffs rise from the sea in Pembrokeshire.

The Welsh name for
Bala Lake is Llyn Tegid,
which translates as "lake
of serenity."

measures 220 miles (354 km); the Wye, 134 miles (216 km). Both the Severn and the Wye flow into England and empty into the Bristol Channel.

Wales is dotted with small lakes. The largest natural body of water is Bala Lake, located in eastern Snowdonia. Wales also has several manmade reservoirs that trap water that flows down the mountains. The reservoirs provide water for English cities, such as Liverpool and Birmingham.

A Mild Climate

The mountains of Wales block cold winds from the east. As a result, its weather tends to be mild and pleasant. In Cardiff, Wales's capital, the average high temperature is 71 degrees Fahrenheit (22 degrees Celsius) in July and 47°F (8°C) in January. Temperatures vary somewhat in other regions. Generally, coastal areas are the warmest, and mountainous areas are the coolest.

For much of its history, Wales was a rural country. Most people lived on small farms and in villages scattered throughout the countryside. Since the mid-seventeenth century, though, a few cities emerged with the development of the iron and coal industries. Like the Welsh capital of Cardiff, with a population of about 346,000, they are mostly clustered in southern Wales.

Home to about 182,000, Swansea (below) is Wales's second-largest city. It is located only about 35 miles (56 km) northwest of Cardiff. Sitting on the shore of Bristol Bay, Swansea is known for its lively waterfront. A leading attraction in Swansea is the Dylan Thomas Centre, which honors Wales's most famous poet.

With about 130,000 residents, the city of Newport (right) lies to Cardiff's northeast. It is a manufacturing center that produces chemicals, aluminum, and paper. Newport's Riverfront Arts Centre has showcased a

variety of music, dance, drama, and comedy performances since opening in 2004. On the outskirts of the city is Tredegar House. The mansion, built in the 1600s, was the home of a noble Welsh family. The house and nearby gardens are now open to the public.

Merthyr Tydfil was named for St. Tydfil, who died there in the fifth century. The city was once an important center for the iron and coal industries. The mines have closed, but Merthyr Tydfil remains a vibrant city with a population of approximately 44,000. In addition to enjoying the city's scenic nature trails, residents and visitors can take a vintage steam train into nearby Brecon Beacons, one of Wales's three national parks.

A woman stands behind one of the many waterfalls at Brecon Beacons National Park.

Rainy days are not uncommon in Wales. Overall, the nation sees an average of about 50 inches (127 centimeters) of rain annually. The southern portion of Wales is the driest region. Winds blowing off the Atlantic Ocean often bring rain to the mountains in the north. This region might get 100 inches (254 cm) of precipitation. In higher elevations, snow falls about ten days a year.

Preserving Wales's Natural Beauty

The Welsh people are justifiably proud of their country's natural beauty and are eager to see its lands preserved and protected. Almost 20 percent of Wales is designated as national parklands. Of the United Kingdom's fifteen national parks, three are located in Wales. These parks include many towns and villages. More than eighty thousand Welsh people are lucky enough to

live amid the gorgeous scenery of a national park.

The largest park is Snowdonia National Park in the northwest. It features hiking paths, bike trails, and a railway that takes visitors to the summit of Mount Snowdon. In southeastern Wales, the Brecon Beacons National Park is known for its picturesque caves, gorges, and waterfalls. The Pembrokeshire Coast National Park in the southwest is celebrated as one of the greatest coastal parks in the world. Its attractions include its sandy beaches, secluded coves, and rugged cliffs.

The British government also recognizes five places in Wales as Areas of Outstanding Natural Beauty: the Anglesey coast, the Gower Peninsula, the Llyn Peninsula, the Wye Valley, and the Clwydian mountain range and Dee Valley. The natural landscapes and wildlife in these areas are protected by law from destruction or development.

A hiker enjoys the view from atop a ledge in Snowdonia National Park. More than four million people visit the park every year.

CHAPTER 3

Living Things

THE COUNTRYSIDE OF WALES IS RICH IN PLANT AND animal life. Its forests, grasslands, mountains, and shores are ideal habitats for a wide range of living things.

More than one thousand types of plants grow in Wales. A few of them are found nowhere else. For instance, Ley's whitebeam is a tree found only on two limestone cliffs in the Brecon Beacons, making it Wales's rarest tree. There are now about sixteen Ley's whitebeams alive in the wild.

Opposite: **Heather covers a stretch of land along the coast in southern Wales. A hardy plant that can thrive in poor soil, heather is the dominant plant in open areas of Wales.**

The Snowdon Lily

For more than ten thousand years, the Snowdon lily has grown in Snowdonia in northwest Wales. This plant thrives on the cold mountain slopes in the region. Technically, it is a spiderwort plant, not a lily. It got its named from the lilylike white flowers that it sprouts in early summer. The rest of the year, the plant looks like shoots of grass.

The Snowdon lily now faces dual threats. As the earth's temperatures warm, the plant may soon not be able to survive in its natural habitat. Conservationists also worry about careless mountain climbers stomping on the plants that remain in wilderness areas.

Forests and Grasslands

Several thousand years ago, much of Wales was covered with forests. Native trees included birches, oaks, junipers, and elms. Over time, though, the forests were cleared to make way first for grazing lands for animals and later for mines and industry.

Today, woodlands make up only about 14 percent of Wales. Most of these forests were recently planted with Sitka spruce, a non-native tree. The largest woodland area with trees native to Wales is the Pengelli Forest. Located in western Wales, it has been filled with oak trees since ancient times.

Grass covers much of the countryside where forests once stood. These grasslands are full of colorful wildflowers such as cowslips, bluebells, and orchids. Other flowering plants of Wales include the butterwort, which grows in the wet grasslands of the southwest. It consumes insects it traps with its sticky leaves. The mountainous region of Snowdonia is adorned with purple saxifrage. This plant's tight clusters of flowers add a dash of color to the chilly rock faces there.

The Daffodil and the Leek

Every March 1, the Welsh celebrate St. David's Day, which honors the patron saint of Wales. Many people mark the day by pinning a daffodil to their lapel. These bright yellow flowers bloom each spring just in time for the St. David's Day festivities. In recent times, the daffodil has become a beloved symbol of Wales.

But another plant—the leek—has an even longer association with the Welsh people. The bulb of the leek is a vegetable with an onion-like bite often used in Welsh cooking. Legend holds that, in the sixth century, St. David told a group of Welsh soldiers preparing to fight the Saxons to wear a leek on their clothing. In the heat of battle, the leeks would help them tell their fellow Welsh from their enemies.

Although the story might not be true, some people choose to wear a leek to celebrate St. David's Day. Traditionally, Welsh soldiers also honor the saint each year by eating an entire leek raw.

Beasts, Large and Small

Of all the animals of Wales, the one most important to its economy is the sheep. Wales's grasslands are ideal grazing grounds. The sheep population has exploded in recent years. It is now almost ten million—more than three sheep for every person!

In addition to sheep, many farmers in Wales also raise cattle. The country is particularly well known for one breed—the Welsh black. The only cattle breed native to Wales, these black-furred animals have distinctive white horns with black tips. Their tasty meat and milk are prized by chefs.

Several other large mammals live wild in the Welsh

Coastal waters are also rich with shellfish such as oysters and mussels. The coast of the Gower Peninsula is known for the abundance of small shellfish called cockles. Fried cockles are often part of a traditional Welsh breakfast.

Reptiles, Insects, and Birds

The countryside of Wales is home to frogs, toads, newts, and lizards. Two species of snakes are native to the country—the harmless grass snake and the poisonous adder. The slow worm

People collect cockles along the Welsh shore. Cockles can be found in sandy areas at low tide.

at first glance might look like a snake, but the slithering creature is really a legless lizard.

The insects of Wales include the southern damselfly of the Pengelli Forest, the great green bush cricket of the Gower Peninsula, and the rainbow leaf beetle of Snowdonia. The holly blue butterfly is often seen in churchyards. It lays its eggs in the holly or ivy that often grows on old buildings.

Many seabirds thrive along the shores of Wales. Among them are herons, swans, geese, ducks, and cormorants. A favorite of bird-watchers is the squat puffin. These small black-and-white birds have strong wings and large beaks. Every spring, their beaks turn bright orange to help them attract mates during breeding season.

Puffins feed by diving into the sea and catching fish. They are unusual in that they can collect several fish in a single dive.

The Red Kite

The red kite of Wales has a great comeback story. A few decades ago, only a few of these majestic hawks lived in the wild. But through conservation efforts, their numbers have swelled. A red kite flying overhead is now a common sight.

True to their name, red kites have reddish-brown feathers on their bodies, forked tails, and long narrow wings. They are large birds, but they are light and graceful in the air. They soar and glide with only an occasional slight flap of their wings. The kites people make out of wood and paper are named after this species.

Red kites are scavengers that feed on dead animals, although they also sometimes eat worms and small birds. In Wales, red kites can also find a meal at the Red Kite Feeding Station in Brecon Beacons National Park. Every day, park visitors gather to watch fifty or more red kites slowly dive from the sky at feeding time.

The islands of Wales also have large populations of migrating birds, such as the gannet and the chough. Skomer Island is an important breeding ground for the Manx shearwater. These birds are known for flying low over the water, rarely beating their wings. With about 120,000 pairs arriving each year, Skomer Island has probably the largest colony of Manx shearwaters in the world.

There are also many land birds that fly above the Welsh countryside. They include owls, hawks, falcons, and red kites. The red kite has become something of an unofficial national bird of Wales. The gardens of Wales attract a host of small birds such as finches, yellowhammers, and European robins.

Protecting Welsh Wildlife

In 2013, a report by twenty-five conservation groups set off an alarm bell in Wales. It claimed that farming practices and human activity were threatening many species of plants and animals. The report concluded by calling on the Welsh government to take action before it was too late.

The Welsh government is now trying to reverse these trends. It has committed itself to protecting Wales's biodiversity—the many varied forms of life found in its natural environments. The government is working with the Wales Biodiversity Partnership to create plans that will ensure the survival of all the nation's plants and animals.

Children scramble through a moss-covered forest near the Arran River in northern Wales. The Welsh government is committed to protecting the nation's environment, for the sake of the plants and animals and so that people can enjoy it.

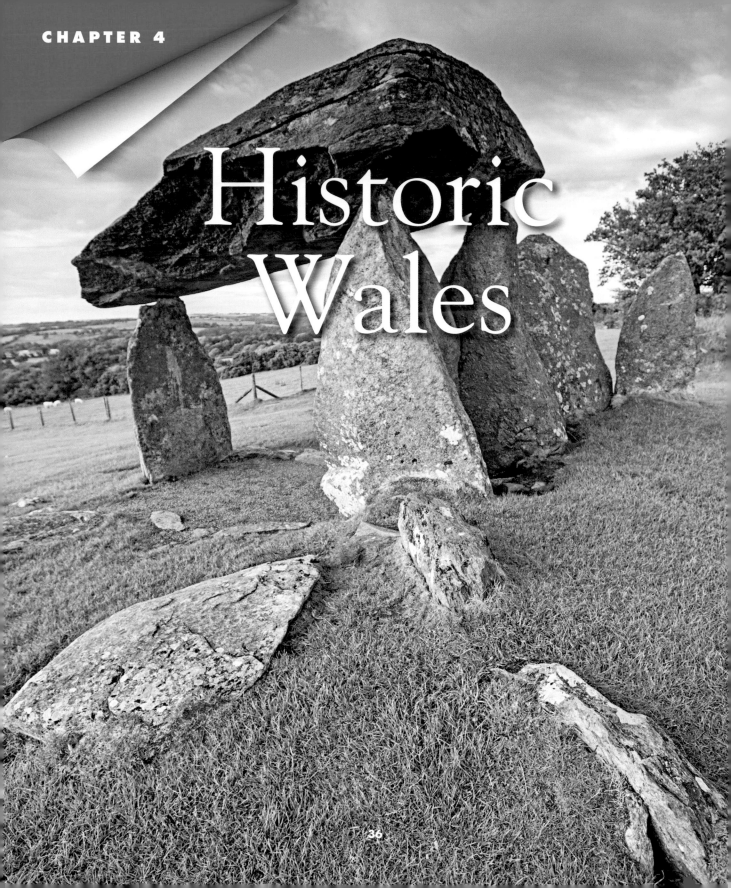

CHAPTER 4

Historic Wales

ABOUT 250,000 YEARS AGO, EARLY HUMANS began living in what is now Wales. The landscape was then cold, harsh, and forbidding. But about ten thousand years ago, at the end of the Ice Age, the climate warmed. The region became covered with dense forests and was much more hospitable to human and animal life.

People in Wales first lived by hunting game and gathering plants. In about 4500 BCE, however, they began farming. As they became more settled, they also started raising livestock and making pottery. Some two thousand years later, the early Welsh learned to make tools, weapons, and jewelry out of gold and copper.

Opposite: **Early people in Wales sometimes arranged large stones to mark the entrance to burial chambers. The Pentre Ifan burial chamber in the southeast dates to about 3500 BCE.**

A detail of a bronze shield from about 2,500 years ago. The Celtic people of this period frequently used spiral designs.

The Ancient Celts

The ancient Celts from mainland Europe arrived on the island of Great Britain about 2,500 years ago. By 50 CE, there were five distinct Celtic tribes living in present-day Wales. Many of the people of Wales are descendants of the Celts. The modern Welsh language also is based on the language the Celts spoke.

The Celts had a very structured society. The common people were ruled by a class of nobles. Druids were also of high rank. They were religious scholars who performed ceremonies to honor the Celts' many gods. The Welsh island of Anglesey was an important religious center for the Druids.

The Romans Invade

In 43 CE, a massive army of foreigners invaded Britain. They were Romans. The Roman Empire had its capital in the city

The Red Lady of Paviland

In 1823, English geology professor William Buckland made an amazing discovery. He found a human skeleton buried in Paviland Cave in the Gower Peninsula in southern Wales. The bones were dyed with red ocher, a brick-colored pigment made from iron oxide. Lying nearby were ornaments crafted from shells and animal tusks. Buckland concluded that the skeleton had belonged to a Roman woman. She became known as the Red Lady of Paviland.

Scholars later found that Buckland was wrong about two things. First, the famous Red Lady was not actually a woman. "She" was a young man, who probably died in his late twenties. Second, the skeleton did not date from the Roman occupation of Wales. It was in fact far older. The skeleton at Paviland was probably buried about thirty-four thousand years ago.

Still, the discovery of the Red Lady site was an important find. It is the place of the oldest known ceremonial human burial in western Europe.

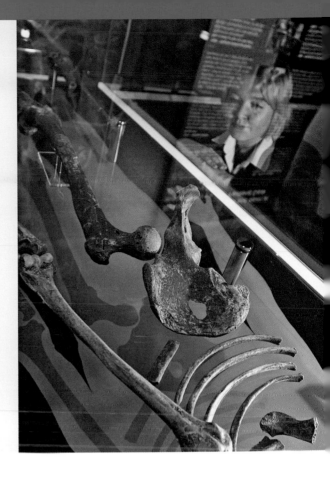

of Rome in Italy. The empire then controlled lands in Asia, Africa, and Europe. The Roman emperor Claudius wanted to expand the empire even farther west. He sent his army to take over Britain by force.

The Welsh tribes battled the invaders. The people of the island of Anglesey mounted a particularly strong defense. But the Welsh fighters were no match for the well-trained, well-armed Roman soldiers. Within a few decades, Wales was under Roman control.

To maintain their power, the Roman authorities built forts in Wales. They also constructed villas (mansions), temples, and bathhouses and introduced new goods and farming methods.

The Romans built a fortress at Caerleon in southeastern Wales. The remains of an amphitheater, now overgrown with grass, are still visible.

Some words of Latin, the language of the Roman Empire, were slowly adopted into the Welsh language.

The Romans brought a new religion to Wales—Christianity. At first, the religion was banned, and some early Welsh Christians were persecuted. But in 313 CE, the Roman emperor Constantine lifted all religious restrictions. The people of Wales were then free to worship as they wanted. By about 400 CE, most of the Welsh were Christians.

Christianity's influence grew even stronger in the fifth and sixth centuries. This era in Britain became known as the age of the saints. (A saint is a person deemed especially holy by the Catholic Church after his or her death.) During this time, leading Welsh Christians, including St. David, established monasteries that served as great centers of learning.

Becoming Welsh

By the early fifth century, the Roman Empire was no longer strong enough to maintain control over Britain. After the Romans withdrew from Wales, several kingdoms, led by princes, developed. They fought with one another for power over the region.

But they also faced an outside threat. Angles and Saxons from Europe began to invade eastern and southern Britain. Welsh leaders, though, fought hard to keep these tribes out of their realms. According to legend, one of these leaders was King Arthur, who is said to have battled the Saxons in the sixth century.

During these conflicts, the Welsh began to think of themselves as a unique people. Even if they were not united under one ruler, they did share a language, a religion, and the same enemies. The Welsh started calling themselves Cymry, which meant "fellow countrymen." At the same time, the Saxons began referring to them as Welsh, which probably translated to "foreigners."

Coming Together

In the ninth century, the Welsh faced down another invading force. These foreigners came not from the land, but from the sea. Viking pirates sailing from Scandinavia began attacking the coast of Wales. To fight the Vikings, the Welsh came together under the rule of Rhodri Mawr, or Rhodri the Great. But this united Wales did not last long. After Rhodri's death, power was again divided, falling to his various sons.

St. Fagans National Museum of History

With so many grand castles dotting the Welsh countryside, the sixteenth-century manor house at St. Fagans, if left alone, might not have seemed like anything special. But beginning in 1948, its grounds were transformed into an extraordinary park and museum. Some forty buildings from different historical periods have been transported there and rebuilt. For visitors, a stroll through the grounds is like walking through Welsh history.

One notable building is Llys Llywelyn, which served as the royal court of a thirteenth-century Welsh prince. Another is the Kennixton Farmhouse, which dates from the seventeenth century. Its walls were painted red to ward off evil spirits. Built in 1917, the Oakdale Workmen's Institute was a social and cultural center for coal miners and their families.

St. Fagans features workshops where visitors can inspect looms (right) and watch contemporary artisans make traditional crafts. It also hosts music and dance festivals that celebrate the unique heritage of the Welsh people.

Wales. As a result, Welsh people could be tried in courts in which they could not understand the language being spoken.

Making English the official language of Wales also made an already growing gulf in Welsh society worse. Most ordinary Welsh people spoke only Welsh. Wealthy landowners, however, were likely to know English. This knowledge gave them more political power than ever before.

A New State Religion

Henry VIII also made a radical change in his subjects' religious life. The official religion in Britain had been Roman

Catholicism, a branch of Christianity. But Henry VIII wanted to divorce his wife, which the Catholic Church did not allow.

So that he could do as he pleased, the king made the Anglican Church, or the Church of England, the new state religion of England and Wales. Suddenly, the Welsh were expected to convert from Catholicism to Anglicanism.

Henry VIII also moved to close the Catholic monasteries of Wales. The king confiscated the church lands and had many valuable artworks destroyed. His actions were a blow to the culture of Wales, where monasteries had been centers of learning and scholarship.

Many monastery buildings fell to ruin after Henry VIII shut them down. The ruins of Tintern Abbey, which had been founded in 1131, still stand in southeastern Wales.

Iolo Morganwg

In his day, Iolo Morganwg was celebrated for collecting and preserving ancient Welsh literature and traditions. Morganwg was born Edward Williams in 1747. The son of a stonemason, he became a self-taught expert on history and the Welsh language.

He began writing works about these subjects, including "Gorsedd Beirdd Ynys Prydain" ("The Gorsedd of Bards of the Isles of Britain"). According to Morganwg, the Gorsedd were guardians of the Welsh songs and poetry of the ancient Celts. Morganwg also revived a Gorsedd initiation rite.

By his death in 1826, Morganwg was revered for his contributions to Welsh culture. At the time, many Welsh people were angry that the English did not seem to respect their language and culture. The stories Morganwg told of great Welsh literary traditions helped give the Welsh a sense of pride.

In the early twentieth century, however, scholars discovered that Morganwg had made up his stories of

the Gorsedd. Even though he was a fraud, Morganwg is still credited with creating a feeling of unity among the Welsh. Today, the National Eisteddfod, an annual poetry and singing competition, concludes with his Gorsedd rite.

The Nonconformists

Some Welsh still did not want to become Anglicans. They joined other Christian faiths, such as the Baptist and Congregationalist religions. People who embraced these faiths were called Nonconformists because they did not "conform" to the state church.

In the mid-1700s, several dynamic preachers began to spread another Nonconformist religion—Methodism. This faith told people to strive to live a moral life and perform good works for others. Methodism began within the Anglican Church but soon became a separate denomination.

As more Welsh people joined the Methodist Church, they built chapels in communities throughout Wales. The chapels became the focus of village social life, and ministers became leaders in their communities. By the mid-1800s, about nine out of ten Welsh people attended Nonconformist services.

Coal mines sprouted across southern Wales in the nineteenth century. In 1840, Wales produced about 4.5 million tons of coal. By 1874, it was producing about four times that amount.

The Industrial Revolution

The mid-eighteenth century also saw great changes in the Welsh economy. Traditionally, most Welsh people had made their living off the land. They farmed and raised livestock, particularly cattle and sheep. Nearly everyone lived in a rural community. In fact, there were no true cities at the time. The largest towns, such as Carmarthen and Wrexham, had only a few thousand residents.

But that all changed when new mining technologies were introduced in Wales. Quickly, iron and coal mining

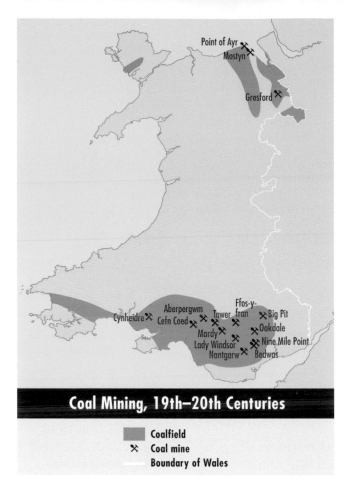

Coal Mining, 19th–20th Centuries

	Coalfield
✕	Coal mine
	Boundary of Wales

became vital to Wales's economy. Mining began in the northeast, but soon focused on the valleys in the south, where there were huge deposits of coal.

Coal fueled the furnaces used to make iron. The town of Merthyr Tydfil in southern Wales became home to some of the largest ironworks in the world. Ships, and later railroads, transported its iron south to ports, where it was shipped to other countries.

Soon Wales's iron mines were exhausted. The nation then started producing and exporting more coal. Coal was needed to fuel the British Industrial Revolution of the late eighteenth and early nineteenth centuries. Burning coal created steam power used to operate the large factories, locomotives, and steamships that were rapidly changing British life.

A New Way of Life

In Wales, the Industrial Revolution produced great shifts in how people made their livings. By the mid-nineteenth century, only a third of the population still worked in agriculture. The majority of men, and some boys, instead became employees of mining companies.

The Industrial Revolution also changed where people

The coal industry and trade turned Newport into a thriving city by the early twentieth century.

lived. When mines opened, workers from all over Wales moved to new urban centers in the south. Cardiff, Swansea, and Newport—today Wales's three largest cities—all developed as seaports that served the iron and coal industries. The Welsh population had been scattered across the countryside. Now it became largely concentrated in southern Wales.

The population also grew larger. From 1750 to 1925, the number of people in Wales increased by five times. Because the mineral industries needed workers, immigrants from many countries arrived during this time. The Welsh now shared their land with people from England, Ireland, Spain, and Italy. Port cities also attracted sailors from around the world.

Fighting Power

Coal mining brought many jobs to Wales. But they were largely low-paying and physically difficult. Miners labored long hours in dank tunnels, breathing unhealthy amounts of

Historic Wales   **51**

Coal mining was hard, dirty work. Miners used picks to cut pieces of coal from the wall.

coal dust. The mines were also dangerous. Accidents were common and often resulted in death.

The living conditions in the towns around the mines were equally grim. Mining companies threw together housing for their workers. The houses were often built in terraces along the sides of the valleys where the coal was dug. Many people were crowded into a single house. The air and nearby water supplies were dirty. When disease struck these communities, it spread quickly, leaving misery and death in its wake.

Miners often banded together to demand better working and living conditions. They staged strikes, during which they refused to work until things changed. In 1898, workers formed the South Wales Miners' Federation, popularly known as the Fed. This union negotiated with mining companies on the workers' behalf.

Miners and ironworkers also fought for voting rights. They were angry because only men who owned property were

The Rebecca Riots

In the nineteenth century, many Welsh miners began fighting for their rights. At the same time, a group of rural Welsh farmers in the southwest also staged an uprising. They were already angry that their landlords charged too much rent. But they became furious when companies started charging them high tolls to travel on roads. These farmers banded together as the Daughters of Rebecca, named after a character in the Bible. Dressed in women's clothing, they attacked and tore down the hated tollgates.

allowed to vote. In 1839, five thousand workers descended on Newport. They demanded a charter of reforms that would give men who did not own property the right to cast a ballot. The Chartist riot ended when police shot at the protesters, killing more than twenty people.

The British government showed little concern about the complaints of the Welsh people. In fact, when it issued several reports about the education system in Wales, it blamed the Welsh for their own troubles. The reports, called the *Treason of the Blue Books in Wales*, said that the Welsh were backward, lazy, and immoral. The report also insisted that their use of the Welsh language made them inferior. The anti-Welsh prejudice of the Blue Books enraged the Welsh people. Many worried that their lives would never improve under British rule.

The World Wars

Despite these tensions, the Welsh fully supported the British war effort during World War I (1914–1918). About forty

People search for survivors following the avalanche of mining waste at the village of Aberfan in 1966. Twenty houses and a school were destroyed in the disaster.

school. More than 140 people died, including 116 children. An investigation of the accident found that the government's National Coal Board was to blame. The board had been told that the situation at the mine was dangerous, but it had done nothing about the problem.

A Government for the Welsh

The flooding of Capel Celyn and the Aberfan disaster inspired many Welsh activists to push for political reforms. They fought for devolution—the passing of some powers of the British government to a new assembly of representatives in Wales. In 1979 the Welsh went to the polls to vote on devolution. But by a margin of four-to-one, the Welsh voters rejected the measure.

Devolution supporters were disappointed. But they did

Supporters celebrate their victory for devolution following the vote in 1997.

not give up. They continued their fight until 1997, when another vote on devolution was held. By then, many Welsh people were angry that the British government, then under the Conservative Party, was not serving them well. With this change in the political tide, the devolution referendum passed, though narrowly. Just over half of Welsh voters called for the creation of the National Assembly for Wales.

In May 1999, the National Assembly met for the first time, marking a new chapter in Wales's history. As Wales entered the twenty-first century, it faced many challenges, from an unsteady economy to a poor transportation system to a lack of good jobs. But, with the assembly in place, the Welsh no longer had to look to politicians in faraway London for solutions to their problems. For the first time in centuries, the Welsh faced a future that they themselves could control.

CHAPTER 5

A New Government

As part of the United Kingdom, Wales is ruled as a parliamentary constitutional monarchy. The monarch, Queen Elizabeth II, is the head of state. But the real government power rests with the prime minister and the British Parliament. The prime minister is responsible for the day-to-day running of the national government. Parliament is charged with making laws that apply to all citizens of the United Kingdom.

Opposite: **Carwyn Jones (holding mic) became the first minister of Wales in 2009.**

The Government of Wales

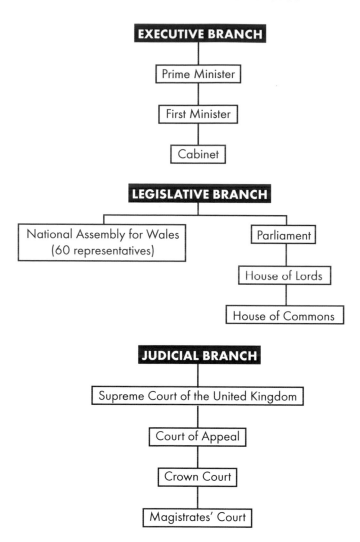

EXECUTIVE BRANCH

- Prime Minister
- First Minister
- Cabinet

LEGISLATIVE BRANCH

- National Assembly for Wales (60 representatives)
- Parliament
  - House of Lords
  - House of Commons

JUDICIAL BRANCH

- Supreme Court of the United Kingdom
- Court of Appeal
- Crown Court
- Magistrates' Court

Since 1999, the Welsh people have also had their own government. Its leader is the first minister, and its lawmaking body is the National Assembly for Wales. In recent years, many powers once held by the British Parliament have been passed on to the National Assembly for Wales.

The British Parliament

The British Parliament meets in London, England. It is made up of two houses —the House of Lords and the House of Commons. Traditionally, the members of the House of Lords were wealthy people who inherited their positions. Because of recent reforms, most of its nearly eight hundred members are now appointed by Queen Elizabeth on the advice of the prime minister.

There are 650 members of Parliament, or MPs, in the House of Commons. Each MP represents a certain area, called a constituency, in the United Kingdom. Wales has forty constituencies, so it sends forty representatives to Parliament. Welsh people go to the polls every five years to elect their MP. Every British citizen in Wales who is eighteen or older is eligible to vote. Sixteen- and seventeen-year-olds are allowed to vote in local elections.

Queen Elizabeth II greets children on a visit to Wales.

A Welsh Prime Minister

David Lloyd George is the only Welsh politician to serve as the prime minister, the head of government in the United Kingdom.

Lloyd George was born in 1863 in Manchester, England. When he was a baby, his father died suddenly, leaving his mother in poverty. She moved her family to the Welsh town of Llanystumdwy to live with her brother.

With his uncle's support, Lloyd George became a lawyer. He won the admiration of his neighbors by representing tenant farmers in disputes with powerful landlords. In 1890, Lloyd George entered politics. A member of the Liberal Party, he won a seat in the House of Commons.

As an MP, Lloyd George became known for his quick wit and skill as a speaker. He helped spearhead reforms to help the poor and needy, including the elderly and the unemployed. One of his most important achievements was legislation that gave all citizens health insurance.

In 1916 Lloyd George became the prime minister.

During his tenure, World War I concluded with a British victory. He helped negotiate the Treaty of Versailles, which formally ended the conflict.

Lloyd George resigned as prime minister in 1922. He remained in the House of Commons until his death in 1945. A small museum in his hometown of Llanystumdwy commemorates his life and work.

Candidates for MP may run as independents, but most belong to a political party. In the 2017 parliamentary election, the Welsh Labour Party—long the most popular political party in Wales—won twenty-eight seats in the House of Commons. Other Welsh political parties that sent MPs to London were the Welsh Conservative Party (eight) and Plaid Cymru (four).

The parliamentary election also determines who becomes prime minister. Voters do not choose the prime minister directly. Instead, he or she is the leader of the party with the most MPs. Only once in the history of the United Kingdom has a Welsh politician been the prime minister. Welshman David Lloyd George served in that post from 1916 to 1922.

Prime ministers are assisted by the ministers they appoint to their cabinet. Each minister heads a department that oversees certain issues. For instance, there are ministers in charge of foreign affairs, health, and transportation. The Secretary of State for Wales is a cabinet position. This official ensures that the government in London addresses issues and concerns of specific importance to Wales.

Labour Party candidate Anna McMorrin celebrates her election to the British Parliament in 2017. About a quarter of the Welsh members of Parliament are women.

CHAPTER 6

Making a Living

UNTIL RECENTLY, THE MODERN WELSH ECONOMY was powered by coal. Most of its laborers worked in the great mines in the south. But when demand for coal dropped in the twentieth century, the mines began to close. The last coal mine was shut down in 2008, marking the end of mining as Wales's main economic driver.

The Welsh people have worked hard to create new types of jobs to replace those lost in mining. Because of this effort, the unemployment rate in Wales today hovers around 5 percent, only slightly higher than the rest of the United Kingdom. Most people in Wales now work in the manufacturing and service industries. But a few rural people continue to live off the land by farming crops, catching fish, and raising livestock.

Opposite: **Wales has three times as many sheep as people. It is home to more sheep than any of the other three parts of the United Kingdom.**

Agriculture, Fishing, and Forestry

In much of Wales, the land is unsuitable for farming crops because of its poor soil and high elevation. The exception is the southern coastal plain and the island of Anglesey. Most Welsh farms are located there. These farms produce wheat, barley, potatoes, and oats for animal feed.

The grasslands of the Welsh countryside also provide food for livestock. Many rural workers in central Wales raise sheep both for meat and for wool. Cattle, too, are raised for meat, while dairy cows produce milk. Wales's dairy industry is centered in the southwest.

The Welsh government has invested heavily in reforesting its wilderness lands. Its Forestry Commission maintains large forests, which are used to produce timber.

Some commercial fishers ply their trade in Wales's coastal waters. Working in small fishing vessels, they haul in catches of lobsters, cod, and skate.

Combined, the farming, forestry, and fishing industries are only a small part of the Welsh economy. They account for just 2 percent of the gross domestic product (GDP), the total value of the goods Wales produces each year.

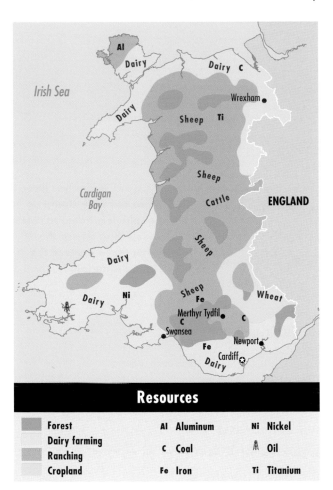

Resources

Forest	Al Aluminum	Ni Nickel
Dairy farming	C Coal	Oil
Ranching		
Cropland	Fe Iron	Ti Titanium

Welsh lobstermen remove a crab from a trap. The trap will then be baited with fish and returned to the sea.

Making Goods

When the coal mines were shutting down, Wales tried to encourage companies to move manufacturing plants there. Manufacturing now makes up about one-third of the economy.

Several automobile companies, including Ford and Toyota, have factories in Wales. Workers manufacture engines and other car parts. In 2016, the British luxury car brand Aston Martin chose Wales as the site of a factory to produce SUVs. Now about seventeen thousand people in Wales work in automotive manufacturing.

Other important manufacturing products include optoelectronics. Welsh factories in this industry make lasers, sensors, solar cells, and fiber optics. Plants in Wales also produce chemicals, plastics, and metals such as tinplate and steel.

What Wales Grows, Makes, and Mines

AGRICULTURE (2015)

Wheat	1,764,000 metric tons
Mutton and lamb	64,672 metric tons
Eggs	532,000,000 eggs

MANUFACTURING

Cement (2013)	400,000 metric tons
Iron (2016)	3,470,000 metric tons
Steel (2016)	4,480,000 metric tons

MINING (2013)

Coal	2,400,000 metric tons
Crushed rock	12,300,000 metric tons
Sand and gravel	1,700,000 metric tons

Service and Tourism Jobs

The majority of Welsh workers hold jobs in service industries. They work in retail sales, education, health care, and government, among other fields. Wales is working to expand its financial and insurance industries, but they are growing slowly.

Many service jobs are part of the tourism industry. About one hundred thousand people work at hotels, restaurants, museums, and attractions. Visitors to Wales now spend about $6.5 billion there each year. Many come from other places in the United Kingdom, especially London. But Wales also attracts international tourists from the United States, Canada, and other countries in Europe.

Tourists often travel to Wales to bask in its natural beauty. Wales's three national parks are popular destinations. The coastline also attracts visitors with its dramatic cliffs and sandy beaches. Dedicated hikers can take in the sights of the Wales Coast Path, which meanders along 870 miles (1,400 km) of coastline.

Wales's historic buildings are also a draw. The nation has some six hundred castles—some left in ruins, but others restored to their original glory. All have fascinating stories that hold special appeal to history buffs. Visitors are also attracted to the beautiful chapels and ornate churches found throughout the country.

A chef carefully assembles a dish at his restaurant in western Wales. Many Welsh restaurants are attracting visitors by showcasing local ingredients.

Wales and the European Union

Another important aspect of Wales's economy is the United Kingdom's membership in the European Union (EU). The EU is an international organization made up of many European countries. Members of the EU can freely trade goods with one

With the decline of the mineral industries, many Welsh mines were abandoned. Recently, several have been revamped as tourist attractions. For example, an old slate mine in northern Wales has been transformed into Bounce Below. Outfitted in jumpsuits and helmets, visitors take a train deep into the underground mine. There, giant nets are installed, creating enormous trampolines. The trampolines are connected by slides that send guests flying from one level to another. While everyone bounces and slides, an LED light show fills the strange cavernous playground with bright, pulsating colors.

another. EU citizens also can easily move to any EU country and work there.

For Wales, belonging to the EU has had some major economic benefits. Because of the free trade agreements, companies from all over Europe have made business investments in Wales. Wales also receives sizable funding from the EU. In 2016, Wales paid £414 million ($548 million) into the EU, but it got back £658 million ($870 million). EU funds help to support many poorer communities. About 80 percent of rural farmers are kept afloat by money they receive from the EU.

Brexit and Beyond

In recent years, some British people began to feel that belonging to the European Union was hurting their economy, not helping it. Others were not comfortable with immigrants from other European nations coming to the United Kingdom. The United Kingdom held a referendum, or vote, on whether or

Money Facts

Like the other nations of the United Kingdom, the basic unit of currency in Wales is the British pound (£), which is divided into one hundred pence (p). Bank notes are available in four denominations: £5, £10, £20, and £50. Coins come in values of 1p, 2p, 5p, 10p, 20p, 50p, £1, and £2. In 2017, £1 equaled US$1.30, and US$1.00 equaled 77p.

British banknotes are issued by the Bank of England in London. Most feature portraits of famous English people of the past, such as scientist Charles Darwin and writer Jane Austen. Recently, some Welsh politicians have called on the British Parliament to allow banks in Wales to print their own currency with pictures of Welsh personalities and landmarks.

not the UK should remain in the European Union.

Carwyn Jones, Wales's first minister, campaigned against Brexit—the nickname for a British exit from the EU. But when the vote was taken on June 23, 2016, 53 percent of the Welsh voted to leave. The English also voted to leave, while Scotland and Northern Ireland voted to remain. The total vote in favor of exiting the European Union was high enough that the referendum passed.

The outcome was a surprise, and the economic consequences of the Brexit vote are not clear. As the British government negotiates its EU exit, many Welsh people are worrying about Wales's economic future. Will foreign companies stop investing in Wales? Will goods exported by Wales be subject to high taxes? Will the British government step up to replace the EU funds Wales will lose? In the coming years, Brexit is likely to reshape Wales's economy, but exactly how is not yet known.

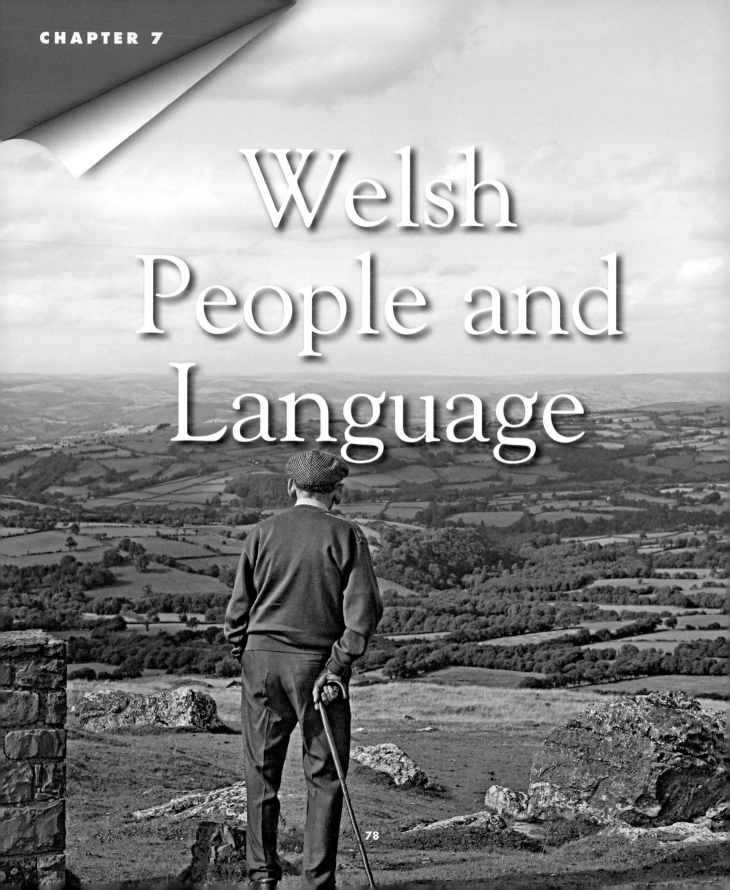

CHAPTER 7

Welsh People and Language

ROUGHLY THREE MILLION PEOPLE LIVE IN WALES. About four out of five of them live in urban areas. Most of the population is clustered in the northeast and in the south. The rest of Wales is sparsely populated.

Opposite: **An elderly Welsh man looks out over the landscape. On average, Welsh people live eighty years.**

Natives and Immigrants

Most of the Welsh—about 73 percent—were born in Wales. Another 21 percent were originally from England. Only 1 percent was born in Scotland or Northern Ireland.

The number of foreign-born residents of Wales almost doubled between 2001 and 2011, so that about 5 percent of the population was born outside of the United Kingdom. Most of the recent immigrants are from Poland. Others came from India, Germany, South Africa, and the Republic of Ireland.

The overwhelming majority—about 96 percent—of the Welsh are white. Some are descendants of prehistoric people who arrived in Wales from other areas of Europe. Others

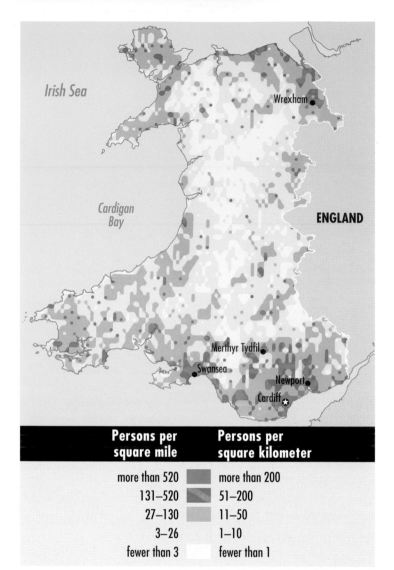

Persons per square mile		Persons per square kilometer
more than 520		more than 200
131–520		51–200
27–130		11–50
3–26		1–10
fewer than 3		fewer than 1

Population of Major Cities (2015 est.)

Cardiff	345,810
Swansea	182,361
Newport	130,086
Wrexham	62,487
Merthyr Tydfil	44,265

trace their roots to one or more groups that came to Wales later. These peoples included the Celts, Romans, Anglo-Saxons, Vikings, Normans, and English.

Wales's small non-white population includes about sixty-seven thousand people of Asian ancestry and eighteen thousand of African and Caribbean descent. Historically, the most multiethnic area in Wales is a neighborhood in Cardiff called Butetown. Also known as Tiger Bay, it was the home of sailors from around the world during Wales's coal boom.

The Importance of Welsh

In the sixteenth century, King Henry VIII made English the official language of Wales. But some Welsh never stopped speaking their native tongue. By the beginning of the twentieth century, however, the Welsh language was in danger of dying out. At that time, much of the population moved to the south to work in the coal and iron industries, where English was the common language. Increasingly, Welsh was mostly heard only in isolated rural communities.

Fearing Welsh might disappear forever, activists took up the cause of preserving the language. Founded in 1962, a group called the Welsh Language Society worked to make Welsh an official language in Wales. The organization also petitioned the British Broadcasting Corporation (BBC) to create a Welsh-language television channel.

Some activists in the Welsh language movement took a more radical approach. They vandalized road signs with words in English. In the 1970s, a group calling themselves Meibion Glyndwr (Sons of Glendower) began setting fire to vacation homes owned by English people in Welsh-speaking areas.

The protests finally pressured the British government to act. In 1967, Welsh, in addition to English, became an official language of Wales. In 1982, the BBC began broadcasting S4C,

A white man and an Asian man relax on a bench in Wales. The largest number of Welsh Asians are of Indian descent.

Ethnic Groups in Wales

White	95.6%
Asian or Asian British	2.2%
Mixed Race	1.0%
Black or Black British	0.6%
Other Ethnic Group	0.5%

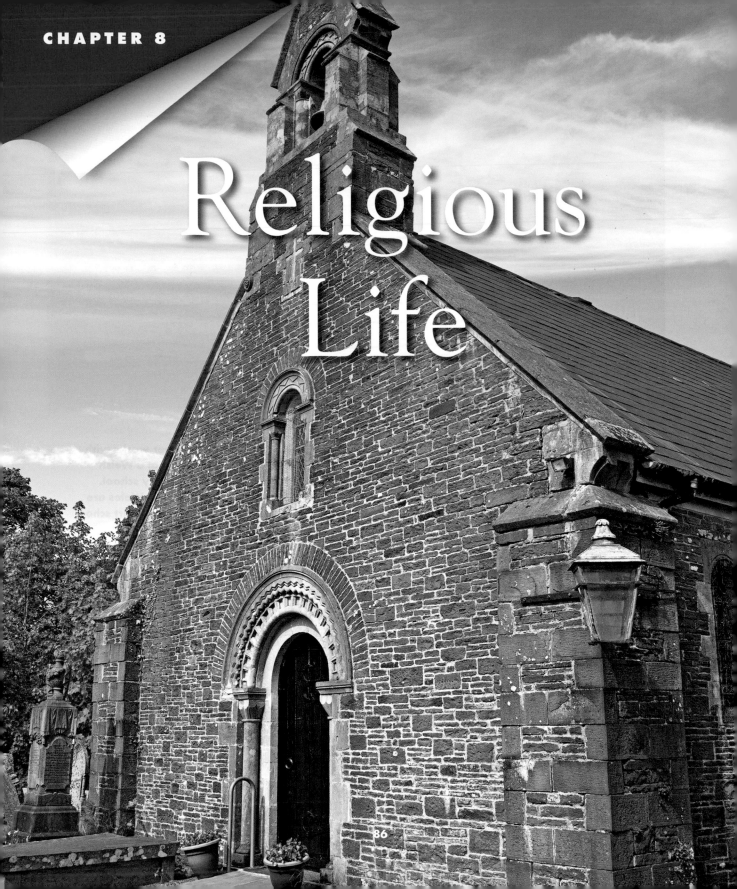

CHAPTER 8

Religious Life

FOR MOST OF ITS HISTORY, WALES HAS BEEN A Christian nation. The majority of the Welsh people describe themselves as Christians. But in recent years, the number of Welsh Christians has dropped sharply. In 2001, about 72 percent of the Welsh people identified as Christian. Just ten years later, only about 58 percent did.

Other faiths are on the rise in Wales. The number of Muslims, in particular, almost doubled between 2001 and 2011. But the fastest growing religious affiliation in Wales is no religious affiliation at all. Almost one-third of all Welsh people do not belong to any religion.

That statistic reflects an important shift in how people live. Welsh communities are now much less centered on churches and chapels than they had been in the past.

Opposite: **Many old Welsh churches were built of stone.**

Wales's Patron Saint

A sixth-century Catholic priest, now known as St. David, holds a special place among the Welsh. As the patron saint of Wales, he is thought to be their divine protector.

St. David was born in southwestern Wales in about 520. The son of a prince, he traveled throughout Britain and Ireland, helping to spread the Christian faith. St. David also established numerous churches and monasteries.

St. David is credited with performing several miracles. His most famous miracle is said to have occurred during a sermon. While speaking to a crowd outside, he raised the lowland he was standing on into a high hill so everyone could see and hear him.

In 589, St. David died on March 1, which the Welsh now celebrate as St. David's Day. One of Wales's greatest churches—St. David's Cathedral in Pembrokeshire—is named in his honor.

Christian Faiths

The Romans introduced Christianity to Wales in the first century. Over time, most of the Welsh became Roman Catholics. But in the sixteenth century, King Henry VIII defied the Catholic Church and made Anglicanism (the Church of England) the official religion of united England and Wales.

Some Welsh Catholics refused to convert. Many were persecuted. More than ninety were executed for their beliefs. However, most Welsh abandoned Catholicism for Anglicanism with little resistance.

The number of Catholics in Wales dwindled until the mid-nineteenth century. At that time, Catholics from Ireland began emigrating to Wales to escape a great famine in their own land. But even with these new immigrants, the Catholic population of Wales remained small. By the beginning of the twenty-first century, about 3 percent of the Welsh population was Catholic.

Today most Welsh Christians belong to Protestant religions, such as the Methodist, Presbyterian, and Baptist churches. During the eighteenth century in Wales, these faiths became known as Nonconformist. Their followers did

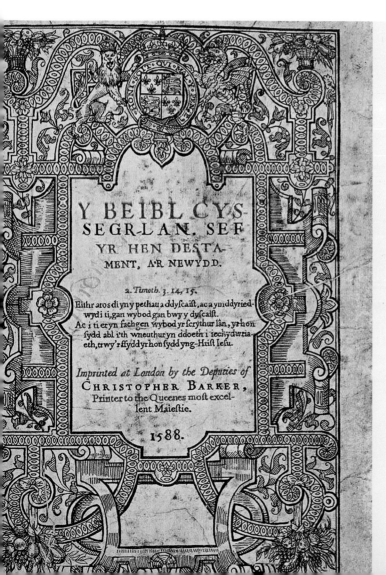

The Welsh Bible

King Henry VIII persecuted Catholics in Wales who would not embrace Anglicanism. His daughter, Queen Elizabeth I, came up with a less violent way of converting Welsh Catholics. She commissioned a translation of the Bible into the Welsh language. An Anglican clergyman named William Morgan spent many years on the project. He made sure to use simple language so that ordinary Welsh people could understand and appreciate Bible verses.

After the translation was published, in 1588, Anglican church services in Wales were held in Welsh. The Welsh liked going to church and hearing their own language. (Catholic church services had been held in the ancient Roman language of Latin.)

Because of the Welsh Bible, the Welsh gradually came to accept the Anglican Church. The Bible also proved important to Welsh culture. It created a standard for written Welsh, which helped keep the language alive.

not conform with the beliefs of the Anglican Church, the official church of England and Wales.

As Nonconformists grew in number, they resented having to pay taxes to the Anglican Church. They supported the Wales Church Act of 1914. The law formally separated the Welsh Anglican Church (renamed the Church in Wales) from the Church of England. Since the act's passage, Wales has had no official state religion.

St. David's Cathedral in Pembrokeshire is one of the largest churches in Wales. It belongs to the Church in Wales denomination, which has the most followers of any religion in Wales.

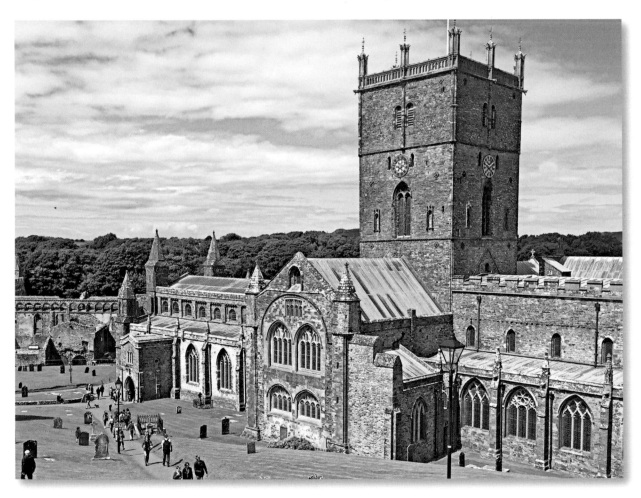

The Sunday Closing Act

In 1881, the British Parliament passed the Sunday Closing (Wales) Act. It banned Welsh pubs from selling alcohol on Sunday. Followers of Nonconformist religions, who then made up about half of the Welsh population, celebrated the law. They wanted people to spend their Sundays at religious services.

The law, which was fully repealed in 1961, did more than curb alcohol use. It also helped create a Welsh political identity. It was the first British law that applied only to Wales. The very idea that Wales could have its own laws helped inspire people to fight for their own government.

Also because of the law, many men founded private clubs, which were still allowed to serve alcohol on Sunday. These clubs became places where working-men could exchange political ideas and organize to demand higher wages.

Chapel Culture

Nonconformist faiths helped shape traditional Welsh culture. In the nineteenth and early twentieth centuries, chapels were the focus of village life. The ministers served as community leaders and as moral guardians. They often delivered fiery sermons, harshly judging anyone who strayed from a godly path.

Chapels were social as well as religious centers. People gathered there to celebrate weddings and baptisms. And every Sunday, chapels were full from morning to night. They held three services, including Sunday school, during which children listened to stories from the Bible. For many Welsh children, the highlight of the year was an annual Sunday school trip to a seaside resort.

Each year, on the day after Easter, chapels held a Cymanfa Ganu (sometimes spelled Gymanfa Ganu), or singing festival. Preparation for the event began weeks before. The chapel's congregation attended a series of practice sessions, so they all could master their singing parts.

On the day of the festival, women and girls wore brand-new outfits and straw hats. The best singers took their place at

Welsh people take part in a Cymanfa Ganu service.

the front of the chapel, so their voices could be heard loud and clear. Then together, the congregation would begin singing in four-part harmony.

The Welsh still hold Cymanfa Ganus at some chapels and festivals. But chapel culture overall has faded. Fewer people go to services each Sunday. Attendance has dropped so low that many chapels have closed down. Some have been abandoned and left in ruins. Others have been transformed into homes, shops, restaurants, and clubs.

Other Religions

Only a small minority of Welsh people observe a non-Christian religion. The largest of these is Islam. Wales is home to about forty-five thousand Muslims, or followers of Islam. Many Welsh Muslims are descendants of immigrants from Yemen, a small country in the Middle East. There are about forty mosques, Islamic houses of worship, in Wales.

Beginning in the 1730s, Jewish communities developed in several cities and towns, including Cardiff, Swansea, Merthyr Tydfil, and Tredegar. At its height, the Jewish population of

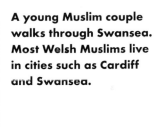

Religions of Wales

Christian	57.6%
No religion	32.1%
Muslim	1.5%
Hindu	0.3%
Buddhist	0.3%
Sikh	0.1%
Jewish	0.1%
Other religion	0.4%
Religion not given	7.6%

A young Muslim couple walks through Swansea. Most Welsh Muslims live in cities such as Cardiff and Swansea.

Shri Swaminarayan Mandir, the first Hindu temple in Wales, opened in 1982.

Wales was almost five thousand. But the number began to drop after 1911. In that year, out-of-work miners in Tredegar took their anger out on the town's Jewish population by attacking and looting their homes and businesses. There are now only about three thousand Welsh Jews, most of whom live in Cardiff.

The ten thousand Hindus in Wales are mostly immigrants from India, Pakistan, Sri Lanka, and other Asian countries. Cardiff is home to Shri Swaminarayan Mandir, the nation's largest Hindu temple. Other religious faiths represented in Wales are Buddhism and Sikhism.

A small group of Welsh people embrace a version of Wales's oldest religious tradition—Druidry. Drawing on the beliefs of the ancient Celts and more recent texts, they look for spiritual experiences in the natural world. Every year, modern Druids gather on the island of Anglesey on the summer solstice, the longest day of the year. Wearing white robes, they hold a ceremony at dawn, during which they make offerings to the sky, the land, and the sea.

Druids take part in a ceremony on the island of Anglesey. The island has been a center of the Druid religion since Celtic times.

CHAPTER 9

Songs, Stories, and Sports

WALES HAS A RICH CULTURAL HERITAGE. Throughout history, the Welsh have displayed a deep love for poetry, storytelling, and—most of all—music and singing. Both because of its strong musical traditions and its contributions to the contemporary music scene, Wales has more than earned its nickname, the Land of Song.

Musical Traditions

The traditional music of Wales features several unique instruments. One is the *crwth*, a stringed instrument played with a bow. Another is the *pibgorn*, a type of pipe made from wood and the horns of a bull.

Opposite: **The harp is considered the national instrument of Wales.**

Pop Star

With a career spanning six decades, Shirley Bassey is Wales's most famous and beloved pop singer.

Bassey was born to an English mother and a Nigerian father in 1937. Her family lived in Tiger Bay in the port city of Cardiff. The multicultural community welcomed people from around the world.

Bassey's family struggled to make ends meet. She quit school at fourteen and began working in a factory. On weekends, she sang at pubs and at variety shows to earn a little extra money.

Audiences were awed by Bassey's powerful voice. While still a teenager, she began playing nightclubs in London. In the late 1950s, Bassey became a frequent television guest and a recording star. She would go on to have more than two dozen hits on the charts in the United Kingdom.

Bassey had her greatest success with her rendition of theme songs for three James Bond films—"Goldfinger,"

"Diamonds Are Forever," and "Moonraker." In 2013, she sang "Goldfinger" at the Academy Awards during a James Bond tribute and received a standing ovation.

vocals. In the 1990s, several Welsh bands made a splash in the European music scene. Manic Street Preachers, Catatonia, and Stereophonics were all part of a musical movement dubbed Cool Cymru. Another important Welsh band from this period, Super Furry Animals, is known for singing a mix of Welsh and English lyrics.

Writing in Welsh and English

Wales has a long literary tradition in both of its official languages. The earliest known works of literature in Welsh date from the late sixth century. Taliesin and Aneirin were authors of praise poetry. They were hired by wealthy lords and princes to write long poems about the patrons' heroic deeds. This praise poetry tradition continued for centuries.

Dafydd ap Gwilym is one of Wales's most famous poets. Writing in the fourteenth century, ap Gwilym composed some praise poetry for wealthy patrons, but he also wrote about his own life and feelings. Many of ap Gwilym's most notable works are rich explorations of his favorite topics—love and the natural world.

Medieval Wales also produced *cyfarwyddiaid*, or professional storytellers. Some of their stories were written down and survived into modern times. These folktales were collected in the *Mabinogion*, which was published in the mid-nineteenth century. The *Mabinogion* presents a mythical fantasy world full of giants, dragons, and witches.

The story of Culhwch and Olwen is included in the *Mabinogion*. It tells of Culhwch, a prince in King Arthur's court, who marries Olwen, the daughter of the king of the giants.

By the early twentieth century, most Welsh literature was written in English, as fewer people in Wales knew Welsh. The country's most famous English-language literary figure is Dylan Thomas. He was considered one of the greatest poets of the twentieth century. His best-known works include "Do Not Go Gentle into That Good Night" and "And Death Shall Have No Dominion." He also chronicled Welsh small-town life in his famed radio plays *Under Milk Wood* and *A Child's Christmas in Wales*.

The poetry of Dylan Thomas is renowned for its mix of humor and sadness.

The Dylan Thomas Centre is located in Thomas's hometown of Swansea. Every autumn, it hosts the Dylan Thomas Festival, a two-week celebration that begins on the anniversary of his birth and ends on the anniversary of his death. Fans of the poet can also explore the Dylan Thomas Trail and see the places that inspired his work.

Roald Dahl is another famous Welsh author who wrote in English. Dahl was best known for his children's books, including *Charlie and the Chocolate Factory* and *Matilda*. Every year, Cardiff, where he was born, hosts a children's party on Dahl's birthday.

Roald Dahl wrote dark but funny books for children. They often featured evil adults who threatened the children at the heart of the story.

Art, Film, and TV

When the Welsh were largely a rural people, they were known for a variety of traditional crafts. These included glassblowing, pottery making, weaving, and needlework. But with the growth of urban centers, many Welsh people also began exploring fine arts, such as painting and sculpture.

A painting of a village by Kyffin Williams

One of best regarded Welsh artists is Ceri Richards. He was especially known for his paintings and drawings based on the works of Dylan Thomas. Another is Shani Rhys James, who is heralded for her haunting self-portraits. Perhaps the most famous Welsh painter is Kyffin Williams. A resident of the island of Anglesey, he was celebrated for his works depicting the landscapes of northern Wales.

The natural beauty of Wales has inspired many filmmakers to make movies there. *King Arthur: Legend of the Sword*, *Snow White and the Huntsman*, and *Captain America: The First Avenger* are just a few of the recent films that showcase the nation's countryside.

Many of Britain's most popular television shows are also filmed in Wales. Among them are the long-running science-fiction hit *Dr. Who* and its two spin-offs, *Torchwood* and *Class*. Another acclaimed Welsh-based show is the sitcom *Gavin and Stacey*, which was written by and stars Welsh actress Ruth Jones.

Wales has contributed many talented actors to the world of film and television. They include Richard Burton, Anthony Hopkins, Michael Sheen, and Catherine Zeta-Jones. The Welsh film industry is small, but it has produced several notable film-makers, such as Justin Kerrigan and Sara Sugarman. Most Welsh films are made in English, but two Welsh-language films—*Hedd*

The cast and crew of *Dr. Who* prepare to film a scene on a beach in Wales. The show has been filming in Cardiff and the surrounding area since 2005.

Wyn and *Solomon a Gaenor*—have been nominated for the Academy Award for Best Foreign Language Movie.

Obsessed by Rugby

The Welsh are known for their love of sports—both watching them and playing them. But in Wales one sport stands above all others: Rugby is something of a national obsession. For many people, loving rugby is a defining feature of being Welsh.

Playing on rugby teams is becoming ever more popular among Welsh children.

A Rugby Star

When Welsh rugby fans argue over who is the greatest player ever, one name inevitably comes up—Gareth Edwards. In the 1960s and 1970s, when Wales's team dominated European rugby, Edwards was its best all-round player.

Born in 1947, Edwards grew up in the mining village of Gwaun-Cae-Gurwen in south Wales. In 1967, at nineteen, he played his first game on the Welsh national team. The next year, he became the youngest player to serve as the team's captain. Between 1967 and 1978, Edwards played fifty-three games for Wales and scored twenty tries—similar to touchdowns in American football.

Strong and agile, Edwards had a career full of game-changing moments. The most dramatic came in 1973, when Edwards was playing on a British invitational team known as the Barbarians. The Barbarians were pitted against the All Blacks from New Zealand. In a breathtaking play, Edwards carried the ball thirty yards before hurling himself over the touchline. Often merely referred to as "that try," Edwards's achievement has been called the greatest try in rugby history.

Since leaving the game, Edwards has found success in business and as a television sports commentator. In 1997, he became one of the first inductees in the International Rugby Hall of Fame.

Legend holds that rugby was invented at the Rugby School in England in 1823. It was a variation on soccer, called football in the United Kingdom. Like soccer, rugby is played by two teams that score points by moving a ball into a goal or goal line. Unlike in soccer, though, rugby players can carry as well as kick the ball. The ball in rugby is also oval-shaped rather than round.

Rugby teams in Wales now play two versions of the game—rugby union and rugby league. The play in rugby league is

Fans pack Millennium Stadium in Cardiff to watch the Welsh national rugby team play. Most people wear red shirts to match the team's jerseys.

usually faster and rougher than in rugby union. Rugby union is much more popular.

Wales's national rugby union team competes in the Six Nations Championship each year with teams from England, Scotland, Ireland, Spain, and Italy. The national team also vies for the Rugby World Cup, a competition between the best teams in the world. In 1999, Wales hosted the Rugby World Cup at the new Millennium Stadium in Cardiff. Now called the Principality Stadium, it is the largest sports arena in Wales.

A Sporting Nation

Almost rivaling the Welsh people's love of rugby is their enthusiasm for soccer. Wales has its own soccer league. The cities of Cardiff, Swansea, and Wrexham also have teams that play in the English soccer league. The national team of Wales participates in international soccer competitions as well.

Wales is very loyal to its rugby and soccer stars. Legendary athletes—such as rugby players Gareth Edwards and Neil Jenkins and soccer players John Charles and Gareth Bale—are often treated like national heroes. The Welsh are also proud of their Olympic athletes, who compete on the Great Britain team. At the Olympic Games in 2016, they won a record ten

More Welsh people play soccer than any other sport.

medals. Four Welsh athletes took home the gold: tae kwon do athlete Jade Jones, sailor Hannah Mills, and cyclists Elinor Barker and Owain Doull.

But as much as the Welsh like to root for their athletic stars, they love playing sports even more. Many people play soccer on local teams. Others like to hike, play golf, go horseback riding, and ride bicycles or motorbikes. People often visit Snowdonia National Park to go rock climbing and white-water rafting.

Jade Jones (in blue) won an Olympic gold medal in tae kwon do in 2012 and again in 2016.

A rock climber makes his way up a cliff in Snowdonia National Park.

Wales's long coastline also has plenty to offer amateur athletes. During the summer, its beaches are ideal for swimming and surfing. Many people also enjoy sailing and kayaking. To take full advantage of Wales's unspoiled coasts, Welsh athletes have even invented a new sport called coasteering. This physically demanding pastime combines swimming, rock climbing, and cliff jumping.

CHAPTER 10

The Welsh Way

DAILY LIFE IN WALES IS SIMILAR TO THAT IN OTHER modern English-speaking nations. Particularly in urban areas, people in Wales are likely to live in much the same way people do in the rest of the United Kingdom, Canada, or the United States.

But in Wales, some uniquely Welsh customs and behaviors remain alive. The most common is the use of the Welsh language. Although only about 19 percent of the population can speak Welsh, it remains the everyday language of many people living in the country.

Opposite: **Welsh teenagers leap into the sea on a hot summer day. Nearly a quarter of Welsh people are under the age of twenty.**

Rural Life

Most of the Welsh now live in cities. City dwellers tend to live fast-paced lives as they cope with new technologies and a changing economy. The ways of rural people, however, often stay the same from year to year. In many respects, their lives are little different from the Welsh living decades or even centuries earlier.

In rural areas, many people still work on farms. As they raise crops and tend herds of sheep and cattle, their routines are closely tied to changes in the landscape and the seasons.

A woman works in her garden outside her stone house.

Their houses are modest. Often people live in simple stone cottages built long ago. The daily lives of people in rural areas are centered on their community. They tend to have stronger ties to their families and their religion than city dwellers do.

Some Welsh people are afraid that the old rural way of life will soon be lost forever. In many communities, the population is rapidly aging, as young people leave to work in the cities. Shops, schools, and chapels—once the focus of people's social world—are closing as the number of residents shrinks.

Many farmers are also struggling to get by. A few are trying to revamp their farms to produce organic vegetables and meat to sell to specialty shops and restaurants. In addition, Welsh

Few people in Wales attend church on a regular basis. Some churches that are no longer needed have been converted into art galleries or inns.

Welsh Rarebit

One of Wales's most famous foods is Welsh rarebit. This dish combines melted cheese and toasted bread to create a tasty meal. Ask an adult to help you with this recipe.

Ingredients

8 ounces grated cheddar cheese

2 teaspoons flour

¼ teaspoon Dijon mustard

4 slices toasted bread

1 tablespoon butter

¼ cup milk

pinch of pepper

Directions

Use a fork or whisk to mix the cheese, butter, flour, milk, mustard, and pepper in a saucepan. Place the saucepan on a stovetop and turn the heat on low. Stir the cheese mixture until it melts into a thick sauce.

Place two pieces of toast on two plates. Top the toast with the warm cheese sauce and serve.

Laverbread is part of a traditional Welsh breakfast. Despite its name, laverbread is not really a bread. It is a paste made of boiled seaweed. Often laverbread is rolled in oatmeal and fried to make little cakes. It is typically served with bacon and cockles, a type of shellfish.

There are plenty of actual breads and cakes in traditional Welsh cooking. Welsh cakes are particularly popular. These small, sugary treats are flavored with dried fruit and cooked on a griddle. Another favorite is *bara brith*, a moist fruitcake made with tea.

In Welsh cities, a lively restaurant scene has recently emerged. Many showcase special versions of traditional Welsh fare. They also feature delicacies such as locally made cheeses and Welsh black beef. But for everyday dining, the Welsh are more likely to go to a pub. Pubs are bars that offer basic lunches and dinners. Meeting friends at a pub is a common social activity, especially in country villages.

Welsh cakes are sold at shops throughout the country. They are often eaten as a snack with tea.

Going to Festivals

The Welsh also love to socialize at the festivals and fairs held throughout the year. For more than three decades, the Hay Festival has brought artists and thinkers together at Hay-on-Wye, a town near Brecon Beacons National Park. Beyond the Border is an international storytelling festival held at St. Donat's Castle. Gladfest, hosted by Gladstone's Library in northeastern Wales, invites visitors to celebrate the written word by participating in creative writing workshops. A recent addition to Wales's festival schedule, Swn is a three-day festival in Cardiff celebrating new bands and musical acts.

The event most associated with Wales is the Eisteddfod—a festival of music, dance, and poetry. The first modern Eisteddfod was held in 1792. It was based on contests held in the Middle Ages, during which musicians and bards performed before Welsh princes.

Eisteddfodau (the plural of Eisteddfod) are now held all over Wales. Among the most notable is the Welsh League of Youth's annual Eisteddfod just for children. The small town of Llangollen in northeastern Wales also hosts the Llangollen International Musical Eisteddfod every summer. Meant to foster peace, the festival features amateur choirs from around the world.

The biggest, though, is the National Eisteddfod. It is held in August, with its location alternating between north and south Wales. Each year, about 150,000 people come together for this event to enjoy all sorts of music, from traditional choral singing to rock and roll. The National Eisteddfod also features the initiation of new members into the Gorsedd. This exclusive group of poets and musicians is charged with working to preserve the Welsh language.

Holidays in Wales

The Welsh have their own unique ways of celebrating many holidays. Some treasured traditions are no longer widely practiced, and others that had fallen out of use are being revived.

One beloved old Welsh Christmas tradition that is beginning to find a new foothold is the *plygain*. From 3:00 a.m. to 6:00 a.m. on Christmas Day, congregants gather in rural churches to listen to male choirs sing Christmas carols. The hours before the plygain are called Noson Gyflaith, or "Toffee Evening." Everyone stays awake by making and eating toffee candy, playing games, and telling stories.

A stilt walker poses with a boy at an Eisteddfod festival.

Welsh Love Spoons

Hundreds of years ago, if a Welsh man fell in love with a woman, he would pull out a pocketknife, find a block of wood, and begin carving. The result would be a love spoon—a traditional token of affection.

Love spoons were less utensils than works of art. Carved into their handles were symbols that represented promises. A heart assured a man's sweetheart that he would always love her. A key promised her security. And a wheel was a pledge that he would be a hard worker.

A skillfully made love spoon also sent a message to the beloved woman's family. It was an assurance that the carver would be a good provider. After all, a man who could carve such a spoon could probably earn a decent living as a woodworker.

Welsh craftspeople still make love spoons. People often purchase them as gifts for weddings, anniversaries, and birthdays.

patron saint. But, even more than that, it is a celebration of everything Welsh.

In cities, people parade down the streets, waving the Welsh dragon flag and black banners bearing a gold cross, the flag of St. David. They also go to concerts, street parties, and food festivals. Everyone indulges in Welsh cakes, bara brith, and the other delicacies their nation is known for.

Many students go to school for just a half day. To celebrate St. David's Day, classrooms suspend their regular lessons, and instead, students spend a few hours singing songs and reciting poems in a school Eisteddfod.

Children also celebrate the holiday by dressing up in cos-

tumes dating from the eighteenth century. Girls wear long petticoats and tall hats atop frilly bonnets. Boys don white shirts, black pants, and fitted black overcoats. Men and women often pin to their lapels a daffodil or a leek, two symbols of Wales.

The festivities provide the Welsh with a reminder of all the things they love about their land—the stirring landscapes, the proud history, the old songs and stories, and most of all the Cymry themselves—their fellow countrymen. On this day, everyone, English speakers and Welsh speakers alike, greet each other in their country's ancient language. "Dydd Gwyl Dewi Hapus!" they say, wishing one and all a "Happy St. David's Day."

A man dressed in an old-fashioned costume leads a St. David's Day parade in Cardiff.

Timeline

WELSH HISTORY

Celts from Europe arrive in present-day England and Wales.	**ca. 500 BCE**
Roman soldiers invade Britain.	**43 CE**
Various kingdoms emerge in Wales after the Romans leave the region.	**ca. 400**
St. David, the patron saint of Wales, dies on March 1, now celebrated as St. David's Day.	**589**
Rhodri the Great unifies Wales to battle invading Vikings.	**872**
Hywel the Good creates a system of laws for Wales.	**ca. 940**
Llywelyn ap Gruffydd becomes the first Prince of Wales.	**1267**
Owain Glyndwr begins his unsuccessful Welsh rebellion against the English king.	**1400**
The Acts of Union make the Welsh subject to English law and English the official language of Wales.	**1536 and 1543**
William Morgan's Welsh translation of the Bible is published.	**1588**
The Methodist Revival encourages the Welsh to join Nonconformist churches.	**mid-1700s**

WORLD HISTORY

ca. 2500 BCE	The Egyptians build the pyramids and the Sphinx in Giza.
ca. 563 BCE	The Buddha is born in India.
313 CE	The Roman emperor Constantine legalizes Christianity.
610	The Prophet Muhammad begins preaching a new religion called Islam.
1054	The Eastern (Orthodox) and Western (Roman Catholic) Churches break apart.
1095	The Crusades begin.
1215	King John seals the Magna Carta.
1300s	The Renaissance begins in Italy.
1347	The plague sweeps through Europe.
1453	Ottoman Turks capture Constantinople, conquering the Byzantine Empire.
1492	Columbus arrives in North America.
1500s	Reformers break away from the Catholic Church, and Protestantism is born.

WELSH HISTORY

Wales becomes a leading producer of iron and coal during the Industrial Revolution.	**late 1700s**
Welsh protesters as part of the Chartist movement march on Newport and demand the right to vote.	**1839**
David Lloyd George becomes the first Welshman to be named prime minister of the United Kingdom.	**1916**
Plaid Cymru, a political party dedicated to Welsh independence, is founded.	**1925**
The Welsh Language Society is established to promote the use of Welsh.	**1962**
At the village of Aberfan, 144 people are killed in a landslide of industrial waste from a nearby coal mine.	**1966**
Welsh voters elect representatives to the first National Assembly for Wales.	**1999**
A referendum passes allowing the National Assembly to create laws for Wales without the approval of the British Parliament.	**2011**
Fifty-three percent of the Welsh choose to leave the European Union in the Brexit vote.	**2016**

WORLD HISTORY

1776	The U.S. Declaration of Independence is signed.
1789	The French Revolution begins.
1865	The American Civil War ends.
1879	The first practical lightbulb is invented.
1914	World War I begins.
1917	The Bolshevik Revolution brings communism to Russia.
1929	A worldwide economic depression begins.
1939	World War II begins.
1945	World War II ends.
1969	Humans land on the Moon.
1975	The Vietnam War ends.
1989	The Berlin Wall is torn down as communism crumbles in Eastern Europe.
1991	The Soviet Union breaks into separate states.
2001	Terrorists attack the World Trade Center in New York City and the Pentagon near Washington, D.C.
2004	A tsunami in the Indian Ocean destroys coastlines in Africa, India, and Southeast Asia.
2008	The United States elects its first African American president.
2016	Donald Trump is elected U.S. president.

Fast Facts

Official name: Wales

Capital: Cardiff

Official languages: Welsh, English

Cardiff

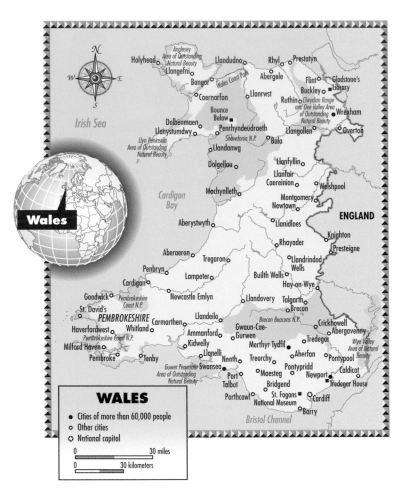

Welsh flag

Anglesey Island

Official religion:	None
Year of founding:	1536 (first Act of Union)
National anthem:	"God Save the Queen" (official), "Land of My Fathers" (unofficial)
Government:	Parliamentary constitutional monarchy (as part of the United Kingdom)
Head of state:	Monarch
Head of government:	Prime minister
Area:	8,015 square miles (20,759 sq km)
Latitude and longitude of geographic center:	52°19' N, 3°46' W
Bordering country:	England to the east
Highest elevation:	Mount Snowdon, 3,556 feet (1,084 m)
Lowest elevation:	Sea level along the coast
Average daily high temperature:	In Cardiff, 47°F (8°C) in January, 71°F (22°C) in July
Average daily low temperature:	In Cardiff, 36°F (2°C) in January, 56°F (13°C) in July
Average annual precipitation:	50 inches (127 cm)

Meet the Author

Liz Sonneborn, a graduate of Swarthmore College in Pennsylvania, lives in Brooklyn, New York. She has written more than one hundred books for adults and young readers, specializing in American and world history and biography. Her books include *The Ancient Aztecs*, *The Mexican-American War*, *The American West*, and *A to Z of American Indian Women*. Sonneborn is also the author of numerous volumes for the Enchantment of the World Series, including *Mexico*, *North Korea*, *Pakistan*, *France*, and *Tibet*.

Photo Credits